YOUR KNOWLEDGE HAS VALUE

- We will publish your bachelor's and master's thesis, essays and papers

- Your own eBook and book - sold worldwide in all relevant shops

- Earn money with each sale

Upload your text at www.GRIN.com and publish for free

Klaus Schütz

Aus der Reihe: e-fellows.net stipendiaten-wissen

e-fellows.net (Hrsg.)

Band 489

The Lockheed Case - International Business or Bribery?

GRIN Publishing

Bibliographic information published by the German National Library:

The German National Library lists this publication in the National Bibliography;
detailed bibliographic data are available on the Internet at http://dnb.dnb.de .

Imprint:

Copyright © 2011 GRIN Verlag, Open Publishing GmbH
Print and binding: Books on Demand GmbH, Norderstedt Germany
ISBN: 978-3-656-25204-7

MBA 500

Managing Ethically in a Global Environment

The Lockheed Case

International Business or Bribery?

By Klaus Schuetz

March 15, 2011

1. Introduction

"When in Rome, do as the Romans do" [1] is a saying that exists in many cultures all over the world. Although it is very old – it can be traced all the way back to the days of St. Ambrose in the fourth century – it briefly describes on of the major challenges companies face in today's globalized economy. Should they follow a universal code of business behavior or adapt to the customs in a particular country. A classic case for this question is the Lockheed Case. In the early 1970s Lockheed had serious economic problems. Facing bankruptcy it secured a government loan of $250 million in 1970. In 1972 and 1973, briberies of the Japanese government were revealed. It turned out that the President of Lockheed, A. Carl Kotchian, authorized secret payments of $12 million to representatives of the Japanese Prime Minister, Kukeo Tanaka, to secure sales contracts in the Japanese aircraft market. As a result, both Prime Minister Tanaka and CEO Kotchian had to resign. Lockheed's contracts in Japan were cancelled. A consequence of these incidents is the Foreign Corrupt Practices Act of 1997 that prohibits American corporations making payments to foreign governments to advance their business interests. In this paper, I will discuss certain topics related to this case and show, why Kotchian did not exhibit ethical behavior in his role as President of Lockheed.

2. Ethical Dimensions of Bribery

The opening quotation of this paper describes a view called "cultural relativism". It states that the moral acceptability always depends on the circumstances in a certain culture [2]. So a cultural relativist would say that bribery is not wrong, unless it is considered wrong in a country. In contrast to that, "Universalism" states that objective ethical rules exist, that core universal ethical principles have to be applied, no matter in which country [2]. Bribery can be found more or less in almost all cultures. But even though it may be in some countries more common than in others, it is illegal almost everywhere, also in Japan. The Prime Minister was even forced to resign because of this back in 1973. So cultural relativism is not an appropriate excuse for Lockheed, because the law must always be seen as the ethical minimum. But why is it forbidden? The simple answer is, because it is unfair. It is unfair to competitors, because the principles of fair and open competition are violated. It is unfair to customers, because it harms their ability to choose the best product. It is also unfair to all citizens in a country, because they expect their government to act for their sake and not for bribes. The autonomy of all these groups is therefore seriously violated by bribery.

It is sometimes mentioned that bribery is basically the same as a commission and therefore not wrong. However, there are some clear differences between bribes and commissions. Commissions are standardized and their terms are valid and known to all players, whereas bribes are per definitionem secret. Unlike commissions, the nature of bribery is to give one player an advantage over its competitors. Bribes are also always paid before a deal is close, whereas commissions are usually due after the deal. These differences lead to the conclusion that bribes and commissions are very distinct things. However, because there are some similarities, the FCPA defines very clearly where payment resembling a commission is illegal. It divides bribery into three different forms. The first one is "Bribery vs. Extortion" [2], which means a payment that is forced under duress. The second one is "Bribery vs. lubrication or grease payment" [2], small amounts of money that encourage prompt performance and do not seek an unlawful advantage. The third and here relevant one is "Bribes vs. agents fees", payments from companies to agents for help in doing business in foreign countries. If a U.S. company has reason to know that parts of this money is used to bribe local officials, the FCPA is violated. Because Lockheed's President stated that he "knew from the beginning that this money was going to the office of the Prime Minister" [3], it is unquestionable that an unlawful case of bribery occurred, and not a commission.

3. The Lockheed Case with respect to Milton Friedman

Nobel laureate Milton Friedman is well-known for his theory of stockholder management. On the social responsibility of companies, he wrote the following:

> "There is one and only one social responsibility of business – to use its resources and engage in activities designed to increase its profits as long as it stays within the rules of the game, which is to say, engages in free and open competition without deception or fraud." [4]

It is important to notice that Friedman does not promote the unlimited pursuit of profits. The important words here are "the rules of the game". There are attempts to derive a role morality for managers from this expression. An example for this is Chris Provis with his poker analogy [5]. He says business, particularly in labor negotiations, is like poker, where bluffing is not unethical but a part of the game. However, it is impossible to justify with Friedman bribery as part of the rules of the game, because Friedman defines these rules more precisely: "engaging in fair and open competition without deception or fraud". What if not bribery undermines the principles of fair and open competition that is paramount for Friedman? Bribery reduces the completion for the best product to the competition for the highest bribe and is therefore suitable to destroy competition, as it can for example be seen in Russia right now [6].

4. The Drucker Analogy and Moral Imagination

CEO Kotchian did not try to defend the bribery with ethical reasons:

> "From a purely ethical and moral standpoint I would have declined such a request." [3]

Rather, he tried to justify it with the benefits of the resulting contracts:

> "Such a cash inflow would go a long way towards helping to restore Lockheed's fiscal health, and it would, of course, save the jobs of thousands of the firm's employees." [3]

This supports business guru Peter Drucker's argument that business has been subject to unfair demands from ethicists. About the Lockheed Case he proposes an analogy:

> "There was very little difference between Lockheed's paying the Japanese and the pedestrian in New York's Central Park handing his wallet over to a mugger. Yet no one would consider the pedestrian to have acted 'unethically'". [3]

This analogy, however, is flawed. First of all, he compares the life of a human being with the life of a company. That is very questionable. More importantly, he implies a situation of duress that did not exist in the Lockheed Case. A pedestrian has no other choice than giving the mugger his wallet. Kotchian wants to create the appearance that he had only two alternatives, either bribing the Japanese government or letting his company go bankrupt. He ignores that there are always more alternatives in business. There must have been possibilities to increase new revenues or to cut costs and thus save Lockheed. Werhane's concept of Moral Imagination could be an instrument to avoid such black-and-white situations, where only the least of two evils seems available. He defines this concept as follows:

> "The ability in particular circumstances to discover and evaluate possibilities not merely determined by that circumstance, or limited by its operative mental models, or merely framed by a set of rules or rule-governed concerns." [4]

A different formulation for this would be to "think outside the box" or as [4] phrases it, "to take a step back and reevaluate a situation from another perspective. This would have been a good way to go for Lockheed. It might have helped to find different solutions to their fiscal problems, new products, new markets, a new marketing strategy or changes in operations. There are a lot of ways to bring a company back to success. Bribery is not one of them, as the example of Lockheed shows. In addition to the cancellation of all the Japanese contracts, it lost its CEO, lost a lot of image and was convicted of fraud and making false statements.

5. Corporate Culture and Leadership

It is often said that the corporate culture determines ethical behavior. If ethical values are promoted by the corporate culture, problems like bribery in the case of Lockheed are less likely to occur. What can be said about the corporate culture of Lockheed? A glance into the history of Lockheed shows that the incidents in Japan were not the only scandals. The company was founded in 1912 by the brothers Allan und Malcolm Loughead as the Alco Hydro-Aeroplane Company, which soon went bankrupt and reestablished as the Loughead Aircraft Manufacturing Company. The company filed bankruptcy twice, before it became very successful during WW II and the Cold War as the Lockheed Corporation. It was revealed that from the 50s to the 70s, Lockheed was involved in bribery scandals in Japan, Italy, Germany and Netherlands. So the history of Lockheed is a history of inconsistencies and shows a company that almost always had to fight for survival, if necessary with unethical or even unlawful practices. This makes it easier to understand, why President Kotchian rather chose the "easier" way of bribery to turn around the company than much more complicated restructuring efforts.

Corporate culture is also highly influenced by the example that leaders give. Some even say that leadership is the single most influential factor on the ethical behavior of a company. Did CEO Kotchian exhibit ethically acceptable leadership? To answer this, it must first be clarified, what ethical leadership is. [4] makes it very clear that it is not "the art of staying in power", as Machiavelli pointed out. It also has nothing to do with visionary and charismatic capabilities. Ethical leadership is rather a concept that supports ethical values like freedom and autonomy within the business organization. No rules should be applied solely by authority. Rather, a system of participative management should be adopted that pushes leadership down the organization chart by sharing decision-making and information with all the employees [4].

It is obvious that Kotchian did not apply any of these elements of ethical leadership. He did not support freedom of competition. He did not respect the autonomy of his employees, because with his unlawful behavior, he gambled with the jobs and therefore the existences of his employees. Moreover, he did not engage in shared decision-making in this important issue for the company. So it can be concluded that Kotchian did not exhibit ethically acceptable leadership. Some might even say that he exhibited the exact opposite of it.

6. Conclusion

In this paper, it was shown that the Lockheed Case cannot be viewed under the premises of cultural relativism, because bribing is generally not only unethical and unfair, but also illegal. An equation of bribes with commissions is inadmissible. Lockheed's behavior cannot be explained and excused as a pursuit of profits within the rules of the game, as Milton Friedman demands, because free and open completion, which is violated by bribery, is one of the most important points in Friedman's system. Peter Drucker's analogy of the mugger in Central Park is not valid, because Lockheed was not in a situation that only allowed one decision. If CEO Kotchian had applied Werhane's concept of Moral Imagination, he may have found different solutions to Lockheed's problems, solutions that are both ethical and legal. A glance into the history of Lockheed, however, showed that ethical values have never played an important role in the corporate culture and helped to explain the motives that led to the decision of bribing Japanese government officials. Furthermore, ethical values were also not promoted by the leadership of CEO Kotchian.

References:

[1]   Ammer, Christine: The American Heritage Dictionary of Idioms. Boston, MA: Houghton Mifflin Harcourt, 2003.

[2]   Mendenhall, M; Punnett, B. J.; Ricks, D.: Global Management. Cambridge, MA: Blackwell Publishers, 1995.

[3]   Class Paper: Dirty Hands: A Case Study.

[4]   Bowie, N.; Werhane, P.: Management Ethics. Malden, MA: Blackwell Publishing, 2005.

[5]   Provis, Chris: Ethics, Deception and Labor Negotiation. Netherlands: Journal of Business Ethics, 2000.

[6]   Stott, Michael: Russia corruption "may force Western firms to quit". Moscow: Reuters, March 15, 2010.
http://www.reuters.com/article/2010/03/15/us-russia-corruption-idUSTRE62E1SU20100315 (accessed March 15, 2010)